ISAAC ASIMOV'S
Library of the Universe

Our Solar System

by Isaac Asimov

Gareth Stevens Publishing
Milwaukee

Library of Congress Cataloging-in-Publication Data

Asimov, Isaac, 1920-
  Our solar system.

  (Isaac Asimov's library of the universe)
  Bibliography: p.
  Includes index.
  Summary: Briefly describes the characteristics of the sun and planets of our solar system and some of the still unsolved mysteries of the universe.
  1. Solar system—Juvenile literature. [1. Solar system] I. Title. II.
Series: Asimov, Isaac, 1920- . Library of the universe.
QB501.3.A855   1988   523.2   87-42606
ISBN 1-55532-386-3
ISBN 1-55532-361-8 (lib. bdg.)

A Gareth Stevens Children's Books edition. Edited, designed, and produced by

Gareth Stevens, Inc.
7317 West Green Tree Road   Milwaukee, Wisconsin 53223, USA

Cover: © Brian Sullivan 1988

Designer: Laurie Shock
Picture research: Kathy Keller
Artwork commissioning: Kathy Keller and Laurie Shock
Project editor: Mark Sachner

Technical adviser and consulting editor: Greg Walz-Chojnacki

2 3 4 5 6 7 8 9 93 92 91 90 89 88

CONTENTS

Introduction

The Universe we live in is an enormously large place. Only in the last 50 years or so have we learned how large it really is.

It's only natural that we would want to understand the place we live in so in the last 50 years we have developed new instruments to help us learn about it. We have probes, satellites, radio telescopes, and many other things that tell us far more about the Universe than could possibly be imagined when I was young.

Nowadays, human beings have walked on the Moon. We have seen planets up close. We have mapped Venus through its clouds. We have seen dead volcanoes on Mars and live ones on Io, one of Jupiter's satellites. We have learned amazing facts about how the Universe was born and have some ideas about how it may die. Nothing can be more astonishing and more interesting.

❧ ❧

The worlds we have seen up close, so far, are all members of the Sun's family. They are worlds that orbit the Sun, as the Earth itself does. We call the whole the Solar system, because "Sol" is the Latin word for "Sun" and the Sun is the central object of the system and by far its largest. The worlds of the Solar system are quite different from each other, and each is, in its own way, a fascinating place.

Let's take a look at our Solar system!

The Beginnings of Our Sun

Our Solar system — the Sun and its family of planets — has not always existed.

Imagine this: It is nearly five billion years ago, and there is no Solar system — no planets, no moons, no Sun. Instead, there is a vast cloud of dust and gas called a nebula. This cloud has been slowly swirling for perhaps 10 billion years, held together by its own gravity. Then, nearby, a star explodes. A supernova! The blast pushes the gases of our nebula together. That strengthens the gravitational pull of those gases even more, and they begin to come together still more. The whole cloud begins to contract, and as it does so, it swirls faster and faster, and grows smaller and smaller.

Nebula: a hotbed of glowing gases ripe for star formation. In this illustration, stars have begun to form out of the vast cloud of gas and dust.

© Tom Miller

Our Sun as a "protostar": The cloud of gas and dust has begun to contract into a Solar nebula. At the center is a huge ball of glowing gases. This ball will eventually explode into life as our Sun. Here, however, it is a protostar, an early form of our Sun.

The Eagle Nebula is a spectacular sight. It is made up of both brightly glowing gas clouds and darker clouds of dust and gas that show up as black spots in this photograph.

The Birth of Our Sun

Let's look more closely at "our" nebula, the cloud we think started our Solar system.

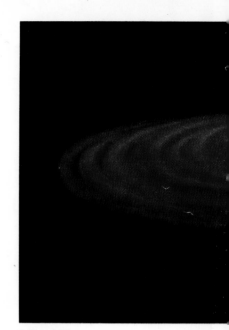

© Tom Miller

The material of this nebula was more than 99% hydrogen and helium, the two simplest elements. These elements were formed at the very beginning of the Universe. Heavier elements made up the rest — less than 1%! These heavier elements had formed during the lives and explosive deaths of stars that were much larger than our Sun. These explosions spread the heavier elements through space.

As the nebula shrank, most of the material fell to the center and gathered into a huge ball of gas. At the center of this ball, matter became very hot and tightly packed. In this heat and pressure, hydrogen atoms collided and combined with each other to form helium.

This process is called nuclear fusion. The fusion released huge amounts of energy, and as this energy spread to the outer layers of the ball, it began to glow.

A star — our Sun — was born!

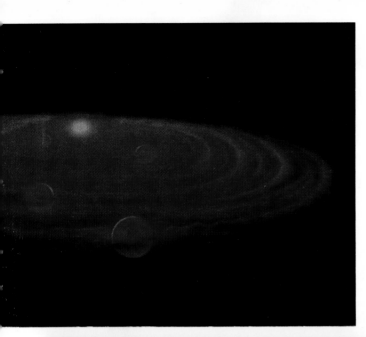

The Solar system as a pizza — of sorts.

Left: The Solar nebula, with the glowing young Sun at its center, continues to contract. The young planets are now clearly visible within the swirling disk.

Below: This diagram shows the paths of the early inner planets as they continue to capture material and grow.

© Tom Miller

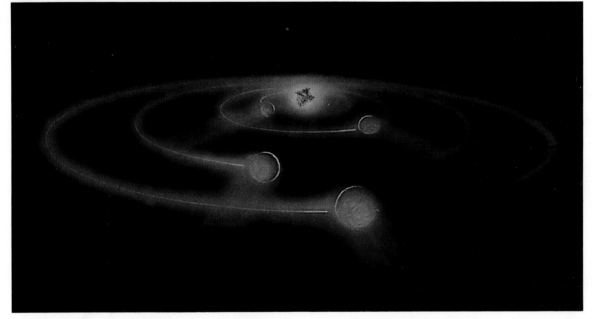

Our Solar system: a cosmic pizza with everything — to go!

All the planets move about the Sun in the same direction. They all have orbits that are not very different from circles. They all move in almost the same plane. By that, we mean that if you built an exact model of the Solar system with all the planetary orbits marked out by curved wires, you could fit the whole thing into the kind of box that pizzas come in! When scientists worked out how the Solar system began, they had to figure out how it got to be this evenly spread out. In fact, the Solar system's pizza-like shape helped lead them to the idea of a contracting and rapidly swirling cloud of dust and gas.

Building the Planets

Away from the center of the cloud, the dust and gas were thinner. This material collected into a disk of hot gases. As the gases cooled, tiny particles began to form. Nearer the center, only rocky elements could become solid particles. Farther from the Sun, icy material could form from the cooling gas. These particles began to collide and stick together, forming larger clumps. Some clumps grew more quickly than others, and their increased mass gave them greater gravity, allowing them to gather more material and grow even more quickly. The rocky planets Mercury, Venus, Earth, and Mars formed where the temperatures were high. The gas giants formed farther away from the heat of the Sun.

Meanwhile, the energy created at the center of the Sun was beginning to reach the surface of our star and radiate into space, along with a "wind" of energetic particles. This radiation and solar wind began to push out the remaining dust and gas of the nebula, sweeping the Solar system clean.

Opposite: An artist's conception of how the Solar system came into its own.

1 (upper picture): "Protoplanets," youthful planets and moons forming out of the Solar nebula that was our early Solar system.

2 (middle): The great "wind" of energy from the young Sun "blowing away" remaining nebular matter, leaving most of the solid particles — and the Sun — that make up the Solar system as we know it today.

3 (lower): Our Solar system today. The view is from beyond the planet Jupiter.

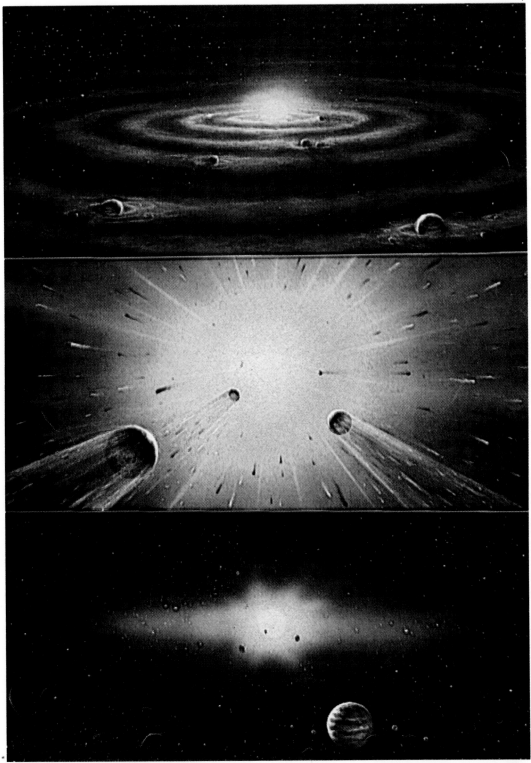

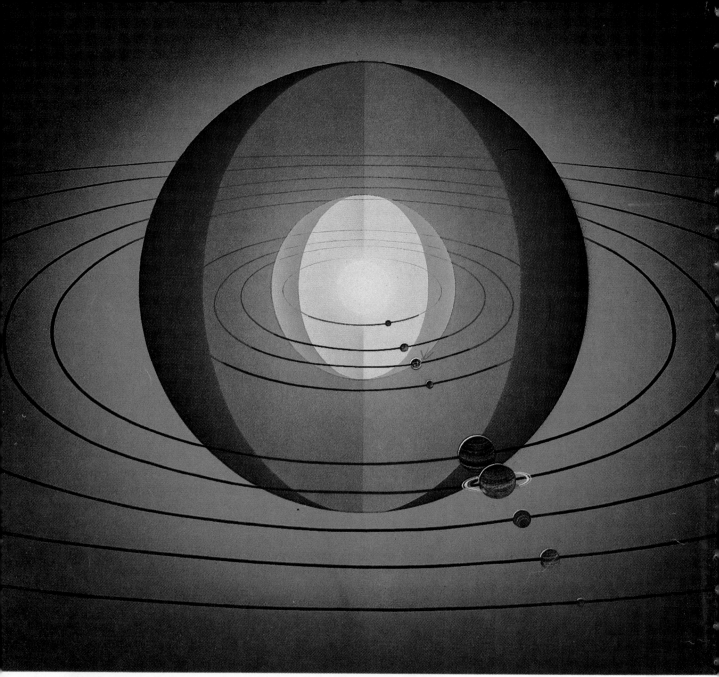

© Tom Miller 1988

This diagram shows our Sun and its family of planets, from the innermost outward: Mercury, Venus, Earth, Mars, Jupiter, Saturn, Uranus, Neptune, and Pluto. Also shown is the Solar system's "ecosphere." This is the area around the Sun that is neither too hot nor too cold for life to exist, as long as other conditions — such as an atmosphere — are suitable for life. In this picture, only Venus, Earth, and Mars are in the ecosphere, which is shown as red. And of these planets, Venus is quite close to the hot zone (yellow), and Mars is too close to the cold zone (blue). Earth is close to the center of the ecosphere, where the temperatures seem best suited for supporting life forms as we know them.

The Sun's Family

As we know, the Sun is by far the largest member of its Solar system family. In fact, it weighs about 500 times as much as everything else in the Solar system put together! It is the only object large enough for its center to undergo nuclear fusion, and so it produces so much energy that it shines. The planets are all much smaller, and nuclear fusion cannot occur at their centers. Their centers are warm, but they are cold on the surface. They only shine by reflecting light from the Sun.

In addition to the larger planets, there are many smaller bodies. Most of them circle the Sun as the planets do, but a few circle the planets themselves as natural satellites, or moons.

Let's take a closer look at the planets.

A companion star? Why not?

Most stars have companions, so they are called double stars. Our own nearest neighbor, Alpha Centauri, is a triple-star system. As far as we know, our Sun is a single star. We know for sure there is no other bright star near it. But what about a dim star? Could there be a tiny companion of the Sun? Some astronomers have recently suggested that there might be one, looking just like an ordinary dim star, and we just haven't noticed it yet!

A cutaway view of Mars showing the structure of a typical rocky planet. The thickness of the crust is like of the skin of an apple compared to the rest of the apple: It's quite thin!

Mercury, Venus, Earth, Mars — The Rocky Planets

The planets that formed quite near the Sun grew very warm because of all its heat. Hot gases, especially if they are light, are harder to hold by gravitational pull than cold gases. The nearby planets could not hold the very light hydrogen and helium that made up most of the swirling material. They could only hold onto the small amount of matter that made up heavier gases, metal, and rock. The nearby planets are therefore much smaller than the planets that formed farther away from the Sun. The nearby planets are mostly rock with metal at the center. They are thus called the "rocky planets," and our own Earth is one of them.

The rocky planets are actually quite small compared to the planets that formed farther away from the Sun. On the left (top to bottom) are Earth and Venus. Just to the right of Earth are Mars, Mercury, and Earth's Moon. Immediately below are Io and Europa (both moons of Jupiter). Below them are Ganymede and Callisto, also moons of Jupiter; and below them is Titan, Saturn's largest moon. Callisto is about the same size as the planet Mercury, and Ganymede and Titan are actually larger than Mercury. All three moons are only slightly smaller than Mars. Io is slightly larger, and Europa is slightly smaller, than our Moon.

NASA

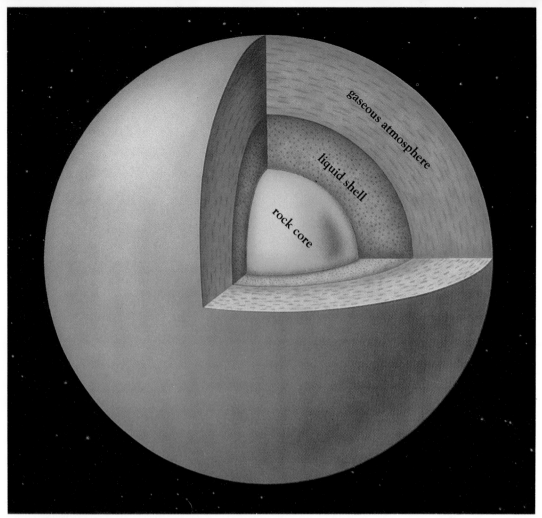

Cutaway of a gas giant: Uranus. Its core is made of rock. Above the core is a "sea" made mostly of water, ammonia, and methane, and a gaseous atmosphere made up mostly of hydrogen.

© Lynette Cook 1987

Jupiter, Saturn, Uranus, Neptune — The Gas Giants

The planets that formed farther from the Sun were much cooler than the nearer planets. The hydrogen and helium gases were therefore cold enough for the planets to hold them with their gravitation. That meant they grew still larger and had even stronger gravitational pulls that could attract still more gas. The outer planets thus grew much larger than the inner ones. Instead of being rock and metal, they are made up mostly of the two gases, hydrogen and helium. For that reason, and because they are so large, they are called gas giants.

The gas giants, clockwise from right: Jupiter (photo), Saturn (photo), Uranus (painting), Neptune (painting).

NASA

NASA

NASA

NASA

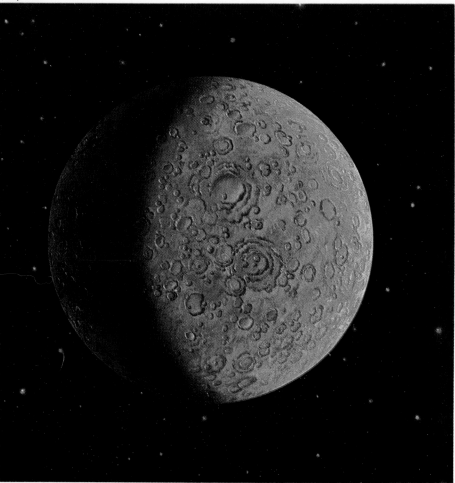

Pluto, a little ball of ice on the fringes of our
Solar system.

Pluto — The Tiny Planet

The farthest planet we can see is not a gas giant. It is an oddball
little planet called Pluto. Pluto is even smaller than the inner
planets. It was the last planet to be discovered, and the dimmest.
It has a very lopsided orbit, so that at one end it even comes in a
little closer to the Sun than does Neptune, the next inner planet.
Pluto's orbit is tilted, though, and there's no chance of a collision
with Neptune. In the last few years we have found out that Pluto
is made up not of rock, and not of gases, but of ice — quantities of
water and other similar substances all frozen in the terrible cold so
far from our Sun.

What next — a tenth planet?

About 70 years ago, it seemed to astronomers that the outermost planets didn't move quite as they ought to. Perhaps there was a ninth planet out beyond Neptune, and perhaps its gravitational pull was making the outermost planets behave oddly. They searched for many years and finally found Pluto in 1930. That seemed to settle everything. But then, as more years passed, it turned out that Pluto was so small, its gravitational pull couldn't possibly affect the outermost planets. Does that mean there is another planet beyond Neptune — a large one? We don't know.

Planet X. Is it our tenth planet? We think it might be out there, beyond Pluto, tugging away at the outermost planets of our Solar system. But if there is such a thing as Planet X, it would be so far away and so faint that it would be hard to detect.

© Michael Carroll

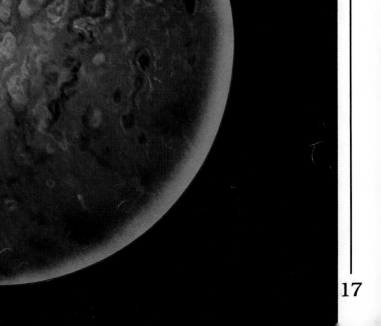

17

Satellites — Little Worlds that Circle the Planets

When the planets grew, some of the material on the outskirts remained separate. All of the gas giants have little worlds, or satellites, that orbit them. Jupiter, the largest planet, has four rather large satellites and many smaller ones. Saturn has one large satellite and a number of middle-sized and small ones. Uranus has a number of middle-sized and small ones, but Neptune has only one large one and one small one. Even little Pluto has a small satellite of its own. The rocky planets are not so rich in satellites. Mars has two tiny ones, while Mercury and Venus have none at all. Our Earth has a large satellite — our Moon.

A study in contrasts: the Red Planet — Mars — and its dark little moon — Deimos. Don't let this imaginary view from Deimos fool you. Mars is close to 4,000 miles (6,400 km) wide, while Deimos is only 6-10 miles (10-16 km) wide.

Left: Jupiter and its planet-sized moons, as photographed by the Voyager 1 probe. They are shown here not according to size but in their correct positions. Reddish Io (upper left) is closest to Jupiter (upper right). Next furthest out is Europa (center), followed by Ganymede (lower left) and Callisto.

Below: Photos of six of the Solar system's largest satellites, shown as they compare in size. Our Moon (center) is surrounded (clockwise from lower right) by Saturn's Titan and Jupiter's Callisto, Io, Europa, and Ganymede.

NASA

NASA

The journey of the Solar system

The Moon goes around the Earth, and the Earth goes around the Sun — but the Sun doesn't stand still, either. The Sun, carrying the entire Solar system with it, is moving steadily around the center of our Galaxy. All the other stars of the Galaxy are doing it, too, so that the whole Galaxy is constantly swirling. It takes our Solar system 200 million years to make one circle about the Galaxy. That means that since the Solar system was formed, nearly five billion years ago, it has circled the Galaxy 23 times.

A time-exposure photo of the Leonid meteor shower taken from Kitt Peak, Arizona, on November 17, 1966. The meteors show up as pinkish streaks that seem to be heading straight for Earth, while the stars make slightly curved trails across the early morning sky. The Leonid showers occur every year, but they are especially heavy every 33 years. The next heavy occurrence should be in 1999.

Cosmic Debris — Asteroids and Meteors . . .

Some of the material in the outskirts of the original cloud did not form large planets but stayed small. This is especially so between the orbits of Mars and Jupiter. There may be as many as 100,000 small bodies called asteroids that are at least a mile across and circle the Sun. A few have been captured by planets and have become small satellites. Some move in closer to the Sun and even pass near Earth. We know them as <u>meteoroids</u> while they are in space, <u>meteors</u> as they enter Earth's atmosphere in a fiery blaze, and <u>meteorites</u> when they actually hit Earth's surface. Very tiny ones might hit our astronauts or rockets out in space, and every once in a while one may hit the Earth.

Planning a trip to another sun?

Before you do, you should have some numbers handy! As you might know, the planets are spread out over great distances. Earth is about 93 million miles (150 million km) from the Sun, but the outer planets are much farther still. The average distance of Pluto from the Sun is about 3.6 billion miles (5.8 billion km). It is about 40 times as far from the Sun as Earth is. There is, however, plenty of room for the Solar system to spread out. Beyond it there are no other stars for trillions of miles. The very nearest star system, Alpha Centauri, is about 7,000 times as far away from us as Pluto is — about 25 trillion miles (40 trillion km)!

Below: a diagram highlighting the asteroid belt between Mars and Jupiter. Also shown are the paths of some of the oddball asteroids that orbit the Sun at crazy angles, as well as the Trojan asteroids — an army of asteroids that "lead" and "follow" Jupiter in its path around the Sun. This diagram also shows Jupiter's thin ring, revealed for the first time by Voyager 1 in 1979.

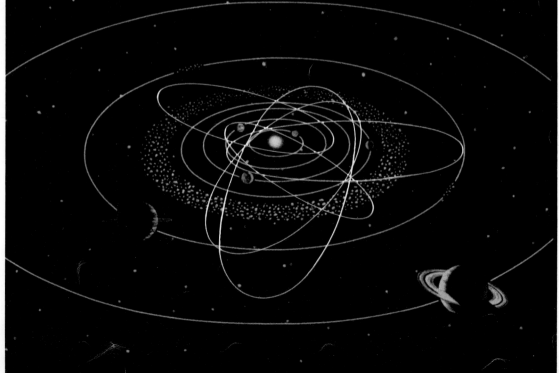

. . . and More Cosmic Debris — Comets

There's far more to our Solar system than meets the eye! Far beyond Pluto there may be a hundred billion small lumps of ice left over when the cloud of dust and gas contracted to form the Solar system. We call these lumps comets. Every once in a while something happens that causes one of them to drop toward the Sun and pass by the planets. The comet-ice evaporates in the Sun's heat. Clouds of trapped dust emerge and surround the comet, glittering in the sunlight. Solar wind, which is made of energetic particles shot out by the Sun, sweeps the dust around the comet into a luminous tail. This tail always points away from the Sun, and that can give us a magnificent view of the comet from Earth.

© George East

© Julian Baum 1988

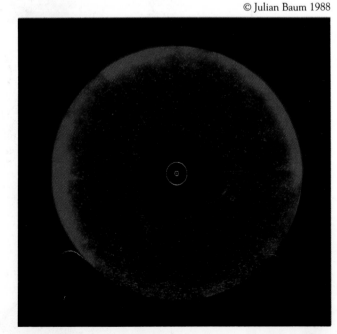

Above: Comet West. Everyone dreams of seeing a comet like this streaking across the sky. But to get such a spectacular view — and photo — you'd have to be far away from city lights.

Left: an artist's conception of a vast cloud of comets (red) enveloping our Solar system (yellow). Astronomers have studied the orbits of comets and concluded that there is such a huge cloud containing hundreds of billions of comets. This cloud lies thousands of times farther from the Sun than Pluto. The cloud is called the Oort cloud after Jan Oort, the astronomer who first suggested its existence in 1950.

© John Laborde

These two photos show the movement of Comet Kobayashi-Berger-Milon 1975h across the sky in one day.

Left: A spiral galaxy (lower right part of picture) appears to lie just off the comet's path.

Below: The same spiral galaxy (upper right part of picture) shows the comet's progress. Also visible in this picture are the "streamers" in the comet's gas tail.

© John Laborde

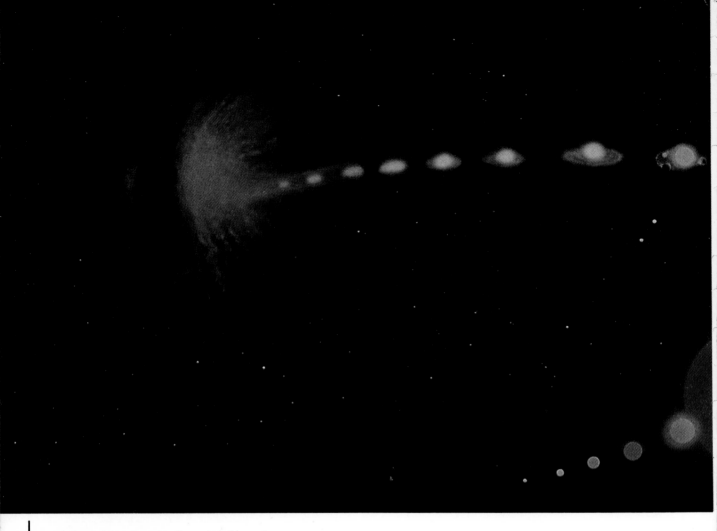

The End of the Solar System

Our Solar system works just fine, with the Sun and all its planets, moons, asteroids, and comets revolving and rotating like a wonderful machine. But it won't last forever. The hydrogen at the Sun's center will run low. After another five billion years, that will cause changes to take place at the center and the Sun will expand and become huge. The outer layers will cool and redden, turning the Sun into a red giant. The total heat, though, will be enough to burn Earth to a cinder, and all life upon it will be destroyed. Finally, the Sun will not be able to have any kind of nuclear fusion at its center. It will collapse into a tiny white dwarf no bigger than the Earth, with cold, dead planets circling it.

What will life be like on our planet just before this happens? Will human beings even be around? Your guess is as good as anyone's.

The life and death of a star.

This picture shows a star like our Sun passing through its life. From the nebula at far left, a cloud of gas and dust contracts into a Solar nebula. The protosun and disk (rear center) take on the shape of our Sun and Solar system as we know them today (upper right). Billions of years from now, as the Sun loses energy, it will expand outward (far center-right), eventually becoming a red giant (lower right). Finally, its store of nuclear energy will be completely used up. It will collapse into a white dwarf (front center) no bigger than Earth, and Earth itself will be little more than a dead, burned-up cinder.

© Brian Sullivan 1988

© Doug McLeod

There is a small white star in Earth's future. Imagine our Earth, and us on it, somewhere in time between the Sun as we know it now (bottom) and the tiny white dwarf that it will someday become (top).

Other Solar Systems?

It doesn't seem likely that our Sun is the only star to have a family of planets. There are hundreds of billions of stars in our Galaxy, and hundreds of billions of other galaxies. And in each of those galaxies, every star is itself a sun. Some scientists think that most or even all of these stars have planets. The trouble is that even the nearest stars are so far away, we can't detect any planets that may exist. In the last few years we have found that some stars seem to be circled by clouds of small bits of matter. Planets may be among them. In fact, in 1987 astronomers in Hawaii made an exciting discovery: a large body that seems to be orbiting a nearby star. Perhaps some day, with improved instruments, we will see just what's out there.

This is a false color photo of the star Beta Pictoris. The star itself has been blocked out so its bright light would not interfere with the picture of a disk stretching out beyond the star. Astronomers think that this disk might be a solar system or early solar system. This would mean that there are, as many suspect, other planetary systems out there — an exciting thought.

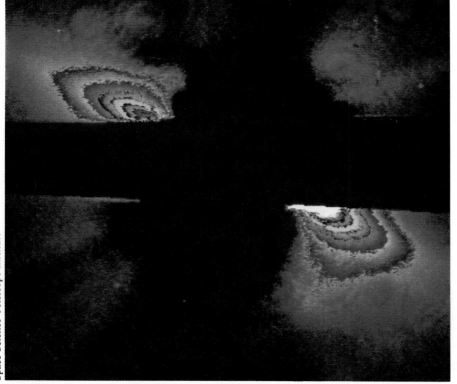

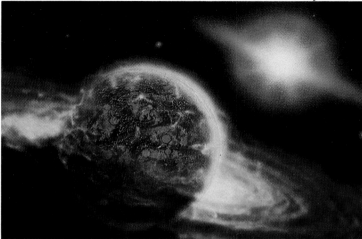
© John Foster

Two imaginary views of planets in other parts of the Universe. Above: planets forming in a young solar system.

Right: two desolate planets in a distant solar system. Beyond them is a stellar treat that is rare but actually exists — a "polar-ring" galaxy with a vast band of stellar matter actually encircling the galaxy itself.

© Paul DiMare

Clouds of comets — stepping stones to the stars?

Astronomers have never seen the Oort cloud — the cloud of comets supposed to exist far beyond the planets. But astronomers have reasons to think the comets are there. If they are there, it is possible they extend outward for over 10,000 billion miles (16,000 billion km), or nearly halfway to the nearest star (Alpha Centauri). Does Alpha Centauri also have a cloud of comets reaching out toward us? It is interesting to imagine comets all the way across between ourselves and Alpha Centauri — kind of a bridge between us and our nearest stellar neighbor.

Fact File: Our Solar System

The Milky Way and Our Solar System: Home, Sweet Home!

For us in the Solar system, it all began in roughly the same remote corner of the Milky Way Galaxy in which we live today. Nearly five billion years ago, our Sun took shape out of a swirling cloud of gas and dust called a nebula. A few "short" million years later, the planets evolved out of the swirling Solar nebula. Today, the Solar system seems a pretty comfortable place.

A view from our perch on the inner edge of the Orion arm of the Milky Way. The swirling galactic center glows thousands of light-years away (upper two pictures). A closer look into the Solar system (lower left) reveals the Sun, planets, and major moons according to their relative sizes.

The Sun from Start to Finish

Here is the life of our Sun from start to finish — from the first contractions of gas and dust into a Solar nebula nearly five billion years ago, to what we expect will be its final form, that of a cold black dwarf, tens of billions of years later. The form of the Sun as we know it — what astronomers call its "main sequence" — actually lasts for only about 10 billion years. This 10-billion-year period begins when nuclear fusion takes place in the Sun, and it ends when it becomes a red giant — about six billion years from now. You can see where these stages begin and end in the chart below. Keep in mind that the ages of the Sun are in millions of years, so 4,700 million years — the present age of the Sun — actually equals 4.7 <u>billion</u> years.

Age	What Happened
(millions of years)	
0	First contraction of matter from nebula into early Sun, or protostar. Early planets, or protoplanets, beginning to form within swirling rings of Solar nebula disk.
1	Hot core of protostar forms from contraction.
70	Protostar contraction ends. Nuclear fusion of hydrogen at core begins. With the "blowing away" of leftover nebular matter, the Solar system comes into its own, and the Sun fully becomes a "main sequence" star.
4,700	The Sun today.
7,000	Hydrogen at Sun's core begins to run out.
10,000	The burning of hydrogen moves outwards to a shell around helium core. As a result, Sun will burn more brightly; Earth's temperatures will begin to rise, very slowly.
10,600	Sun's life as a "main sequence" star comes to an end. First red-giant stage. Helium core ignites. Outer area of star forced outward; Earth's temperatures will be at boiling point.
10,650	Final red-giant stage begins. Earth a charred planet.
11,000	Final red-giant stage reaches maximum state. Helium fusion moves to shell around core. Dying star gives off gas and dust as a "planetary" nebula. White dwarf forms in 75,000 years.
?	White dwarf cools into a black dwarf, taking tens of billions of years.

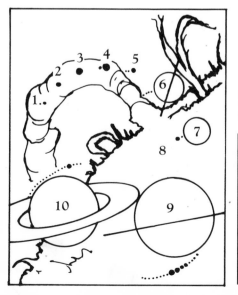

Left: a guide to the Solar system on the opposite page.

KEY	
1 — Pluto	6 — Uranus
2 — Mercury	7 — Neptune
3 — Venus	8 — Sun
4 — Earth	9 — Jupiter
5 — Mars	10 — Saturn

More Books About the Solar System

Here are more books about the Solar system. If you are interested in them, check your library or bookstore.

Our Wonderful Solar System. Adams (Troll)
Planets and the Solar System. Brandt (Troll)
The Solar System. Lambert (Franklin Watts)
The Sun. Asimov (Gareth Stevens)
Wonders Around the Sun. Bonner (Lantern)

Places to Visit

You can explore our Solar system and other places in the Universe without leaving Earth. Here are some museums and centers where you can find a variety of space exhibits.

American Museum - Hayden Planetarium
New York, New York

Science North Solar Observatory
Sudbury, Ontario

National Air and Space Museum
Smithsonian Institution
Washington, DC

MacDonald Observatory
Austin, Texas

The Space and Rocket Center
Huntsville, Alabama

National Museum of Science
and Technology
Ottawa, Ontario

For More Information About the Solar System

Here are some people you can write away to for more information about the Solar system. Be sure to tell them exactly what you want to know about or see. And include your full name, age, and address so they can write back to you.

For information about the Solar system:
National Space Society
600 Maryland Avenue, SW
Washington, DC 20024

The Planetary Society
65 North Catalina
Pasadena, California 91106

For monthly sky maps:
National Museum of Science and Technology
Astronomy Division
2380 Lancaster Road
Ottawa, Ontario K1A 0M8
Canada

Space Communications Branch
Ministry of State for Science
and Technology
240 Sparks St., C.D. Howe Bldg.
Ottawa, Ontario K1A 1A1
Canada

Glossary

asteroids: very small planets and even smaller objects made of rock or metal. There are thousands of them in our Solar system, and they mainly orbit the Sun in large numbers between Mars and Jupiter. But some show up elsewhere in the Solar system — some as meteoroids and some possibly as "captured" moons of planets such as Mars.

billion: the number represented by 1 followed by nine zeroes - 1,000,000,000. In some countries, such as the United Kingdom (Great Britain), this number is called "a thousand million." In these countries, one billion would then be represented by 1 followed by 12 zeroes — 1,000,000,000,000: a million million.

black hole: a massive object — usually a collapsed star — so tightly packed that not even light can escape the force of its gravity.

double stars: stars that circle each other.

galaxy: any of the many large groupings of stars, gas, and dust that exist in the Universe. Our Galaxy is known as the Milky Way.

gas giants: Jupiter, Saturn, Uranus, and Neptune; the farther planets from the Sun — not counting Pluto. They consist mostly of hydrogen and helium, rather than rock and metal.

helium: a light, colorless gas that makes up part of every star.

hydrogen: a colorless, ordorless gas that is the simplest and lightest of the elements. Stars are three-quarters hydrogen.

meteor: a tiny asteroid or meteoroid that has entered the Earth's atmosphere. Also, the bright streak of light made as the meteoroid enters or moves through the atmosphere.

meteorite: a meteoroid when it hits the Earth.

meteoroid: a lump of rock or metal drifting through space. Meteoroids can be as big as asteroids or as small as specks of dust.

natural satellites: another name for the moons that orbit planets.

nebula: a vast cloud of dust and gas in space.

nuclear fusion: the collision and combination of hydrogen atoms that produces helium.

proto-: the earliest or first form of something. In this book, we talk about the young Sun as a "protostar" or "protosun," and about the early planets as "protoplanets."

rocky planets: Mercury, Venus, Earth, and Mars; the planets closest to the Sun. They all have rock and metal at their centers.

Solar system: the Sun with the planets and all other bodies that orbit the Sun.

Sun: our star and provider of the energy that makes life possible on Earth.

supernova: a red giant that has collapsed, heating its cool outer layers and causing explosions.

Universe: everything that we know exists and that we believe may exist.

white dwarf: the small, white-hot body that remains when a star like our Sun collapses.

Index

The publishers wish to thank the following for permission to reproduce copyright material: front cover, pp. 24-25, © Brian Sullivan 1988; pp. 4, 5 (upper), 6-7, 7, 10, 28 (upper), © Tom Miller; p. 5 (lower), National Optical Astronomy Observatories; p. 9, © David Hardy; pp. 12, 16, © Lynette Cook 1988; pp. 14, 21, © Lynette Cook 1987; pp. 13, 15 (all), 19 (both), courtesy of NASA; p. 17, © Michael Carroll; p. 18, © Kurt Burmann 1988; pp. 20-21 (upper), © Dennis Milon; p. 22 (upper), © George East; p. 22 (lower), © Julian Baum 1988; p. 23 (both), © John Laborde; p. 25 (lower), © Doug McLeod; p. 26, Space Science Telescope Institute; p. 27 (upper), © John Foster; p. 27 (lower), © Paul DiMare; p,. 28 (lower), © Ron Miller.